Apple Watch Series 7

USER GUIDE

The instructive user manual for Apple watch series 7 – hacks, tips & skills and more

Contents

Introduction

Brief overview of Fitbit Charge 5

The Apple Watch Series 7 is the latest iteration of Apple's popular smartwatch lineup. It features a larger, always-on Retina display that is 20% bigger than the previous generation, with thinner borders and rounded corners. The Series 7 is also more durable, with a crack-resistant front crystal and improved water resistance. It comes with new watch faces and bands, and is available in a variety of colors and finishes.

In terms of features, the Series 7 includes advanced health and fitness tracking, including a new cycling workout type, improved algorithms for measuring calorie burn, and enhanced sleep tracking. It also features new communication tools, such as the ability to send messages and make calls without needing to have your iPhone nearby. With its powerful processor and advanced sensors, the Apple Watch Series 7 is a versatile and powerful device that can help you stay connected, track your fitness goals, and manage your busy life on the go.

Technical specifications

Here are some technical specifications for the Fitbit Charge 5:

Display:

- Always-on Retina LTPO OLED display
- 41mm and 45mm sizes
- 1.57 inches (39.8mm) and 1.78 inches (45.2mm) display respectively
- 1000 nits brightness

Processor:

- S7 SiP with 64-bit dual-core processor
- W3 Apple wireless chip
- U1 ultra-wideband chip

Connectivity:

- Bluetooth 5.0
- Wi-Fi (802.11b/g/n 2.4GHz and 5GHz)
- GPS/GNSS
- Cellular models also have UMTS/HSPA/LTE (GSM/CDMA)

Sensors:

- Blood oxygen sensor
- Electrical heart sensor (ECG app)
- Optical heart sensor
- Accelerometer
- Gyroscope
- Ambient light sensor
- Barometric altimeter

Battery life:

- Up to 18 hours of battery life

Water resistance:

- WR50 water resistance rating

Dimensions:

- 41.3mm x 34.6mm x 9.8mm (height x width x depth)
- 45.3mm x 38.8mm x 10.7mm (height x width x depth)

Weight:

- 41mm GPS: 30.5g
- 45mm GPS: 36.9g
- 41mm GPS + Cellular: 31.9g
- 45mm GPS + Cellular: 39.7g

Other features:

- Siri voice assistant
- Built-in speaker and microphone
- Digital Crown with haptic feedback
- Emergency SOS
- Fall detection
- Family Setup
- Noise monitoring

Overall, the Apple Watch Series 7 boasts several notable upgrades over its predecessor, including a larger and brighter always-on display, faster charging time, and enhanced durability. Additionally, it offers advanced health and fitness tracking features, cellular connectivity, and a range of customization options.

Getting Started

Unboxing the device

When you first receive your Apple Watch Series 7, you can expect the following items to be included in the box:

- Apple Watch Series 7
- Charging cable (USB-A to Magnetic Charging Cable)
- Power Adapter (sold separately)
- Quick Start Guide
- Warranty Information

The Apple Watch Series 7 comes in a compact and elegant box that is easy to open. Once you remove the lid, you will see the watch nestled in a clear plastic tray. The charging cable and power adapter are neatly tucked away underneath the tray, along with the Quick Start Guide and warranty information.

The charging cable for the Apple Watch Series 7 is a magnetic cable that attaches to the back of the watch. The other end of the cable is a USB-A connector, which can be plugged into a power adapter (sold separately) or a USB port on your computer.

Overall, the unboxing experience for the Apple Watch Series 7 is straightforward and user-friendly. With all the necessary accessories included, you can start using your watch right away.

Charging the watch

Charging the Apple Watch Series 7 is a simple and straightforward process. Here are the steps to follow:

1. Connect the Magnetic Charging Cable to the Apple Watch Series 7:
   - The Magnetic Charging Cable attaches to the back of the watch, aligning with the circular charging pad. The magnets will automatically snap the cable into place.
2. Connect the Magnetic Charging Cable to a Power Source:
   - Plug the USB-A end of the cable into a power adapter (sold separately) or a USB port on your computer. The charging cable is designed to provide optimal charging performance when used with an Apple-branded USB power adapter.
3. Charging Status:
   - When you connect the watch to the charger, the watch face will display a charging icon (a lightning bolt inside a circular battery icon) indicating that the watch is charging. You can also check the battery level and charging status in the Control Center or the Battery widget on the watch.
4. Charging Time:
   - Depending on the battery level and the power source, it may take up to 2.5 hours to fully charge the Apple Watch Series 7. However, the watch is

designed to optimize charging time and will charge up to 80% in about 1.5 hours.

5. Disconnecting the Charging Cable:
   - Once the watch is fully charged, you can disconnect the Magnetic Charging Cable from the watch by gently pulling it away from the back of the watch. Make sure to unplug the cable from the power source as well.

By following these steps, you can ensure that your Apple Watch Series 7 is always fully charged and ready to use.

Pairing the watch with an iPhone

To get the most out of your Apple Watch Series 7, you will need to pair it with your iPhone. Here are the steps to follow:

1. Make sure your iPhone is running iOS 15 or later.
2. Turn on your Apple Watch Series 7:
   - Press and hold the side button until the Apple logo appears on the screen.
3. Hold your Apple Watch Series 7 near your iPhone:
   - Your iPhone should be unlocked and connected to a Wi-Fi or cellular network. The Apple Watch will prompt you to open the Apple Watch app on your iPhone.
4. Open the Apple Watch app on your iPhone:
   - If you don't have the app installed, you can download it from the App Store. Once you have

the app open, tap on "Start Pairing" to begin the process.

5. Follow the on-screen instructions:
   - The app will guide you through the process of pairing your Apple Watch Series 7 with your iPhone. You will need to align the watch face with the viewfinder on your iPhone and enter a six-digit code to confirm the pairing.

6. Set up your Apple Watch Series 7:
   - Once your watch is paired with your iPhone, you can customize your settings, add apps, and set up your preferences using the Apple Watch app.

7. Enjoy your new Apple Watch Series 7:
   - With your watch paired with your iPhone, you can receive notifications, make calls, send messages, track your fitness goals, and access a wide range of apps directly from your wrist.

By following these steps, you can quickly and easily pair your Apple Watch Series 7 with your iPhone and start enjoying all the features and functionalities of this powerful device.

Apple Watch Basics

Watch face and complications

One of the key features of the Apple Watch Series 7 is its ability to display a wide range of watch faces, each with its own style and customization options. Watch faces are essentially the home screen of your Apple Watch, and they can display a variety of information, including the time, date, weather, activity data, and more. You can customize your watch face by choosing a design, selecting a color scheme, and adding complications.

Complications are small widgets that can display information on your watch face, such as your heart rate, upcoming appointments, or news headlines. You can customize which complications appear on your watch face and where they are located.

Here's how to customize your watch face and add complications on the Apple Watch Series 7:

1. From the watch face, swipe left or right to select a watch face design.
2. Tap and hold the watch face until it starts to jiggle.
3. Tap the "Customize" button.
4. Use the Digital Crown to scroll through the available customization options, such as color, style, and complications.
5. To add a complication, tap the location on the watch face where you want to add it, then use the Digital Crown to select the complication you want to add.
6. Once you've made your changes, tap "Done" to save your customized watch face.

You can also create multiple watch faces and switch between them as needed. To do so, simply swipe left or right on the watch face and select a different watch face design.

By customizing your watch face and adding complications, you can personalize your Apple Watch Series 7 to display the information that's most important to you.

Navigating the watch with touch and gestures

The Apple Watch Series 7 features a touchscreen display that responds to touch and gestures. Here's how to navigate your watch using touch and gestures:

1. Tap:

- Tap the screen with your finger to select an item, open an app, or activate a control.

2. Swipe:
   - Swipe left or right to scroll through items, such as notifications or messages.
   - Swipe up from the bottom of the screen to access the Control Center.
   - Swipe down from the top of the screen to access the Notification Center.

3. Force Touch:
   - Press firmly on the screen to reveal additional options and controls.

4. Digital Crown:
   - Turn the Digital Crown to scroll through items, zoom in and out, or adjust the volume.
   - Press the Digital Crown to return to the home screen or activate Siri.

5. Side Button:
   - Press and hold the side button to access the power off and emergency SOS options.
   - Double-press the side button to switch between the last two apps you used.

6. Hand Gestures:
   - Raise your wrist to wake up the screen.
   - Lower your wrist to put the screen to sleep.

By using these touch and gesture controls, you can easily navigate your Apple Watch Series 7 and access its many features and functions. The watch is designed to be intuitive and easy to use, so don't be afraid to experiment and explore all that it has to offer.

Customizing settings

Customizing the settings on your Apple Watch Series 7 can help you get the most out of your device and tailor it to your preferences. Here are some of the key settings you can customize on your Apple Watch Series 7:

1. **Watch Face:** You can choose from a variety of watch face designs and customize the color, style, and complications.
2. **Notifications:** You can choose which apps send notifications to your watch and how those notifications are displayed.
3. **Sounds and Haptics:** You can adjust the volume of the watch's sounds and vibrations, including setting a different haptic strength for incoming calls and notifications.
4. **Display and Brightness:** You can adjust the brightness of the watch's display and choose whether to enable always-on display mode.
5. **App Layout:** You can customize the order of your app icons on the watch face and in the app launcher.
6. **Accessibility:** You can enable various accessibility features, such as VoiceOver, Zoom, and larger text.

7. **Workout:** You can customize your workout metrics, such as which metrics are displayed during workouts and which workouts are tracked.

To customize these settings and more, follow these steps:

- Open the Settings app on your Apple Watch Series 7.
- Scroll through the options and tap the setting you want to customize.
- Adjust the settings to your preferences.
- When you're finished customizing the settings, tap the back button to save your changes.

By customizing your Apple Watch Series 7 settings, you can make your device work better for you and improve your overall user experience.

Fitness and Health Features

Setting fitness goals

Setting fitness goals on your Apple Watch Series 7 can help you stay motivated and track your progress as you work towards improving your fitness level. Here's how to set fitness goals on your Apple Watch:

1. Open the Fitness app on your Apple Watch Series 7.
2. Scroll down and tap the "Set Your Goal" button.
3. Choose the type of workout you want to set a goal for, such as walking, running, cycling, or swimming.
4. Use the Digital Crown to set your goal, such as a specific distance, time, or calorie burn.
5. Tap "Start" to begin your workout.

Once you've set a goal, your Apple Watch will track your progress and provide you with updates and reminders as you work towards achieving your goal. You can also view your workout history and track your progress over time

Here are some tips for setting and achieving your fitness goals on your Apple Watch Series 7:

1. Start with a realistic goal that is challenging but achievable.
2. Set specific and measurable goals, such as walking 10,000 steps a day or running a 5K in under 30 minutes.

3. Mix up your workouts to keep things interesting and avoid boredom.
4. Use the Activity app on your iPhone to view your progress and share your achievements with friends and family.
5. Celebrate your successes and don't get discouraged if you don't meet your goal every day.

By setting fitness goals and tracking your progress on your Apple Watch Series 7, you can stay motivated and on track towards achieving your fitness goals.

Tracking workouts and activities

The Apple Watch Series 7 is an excellent fitness tracking device that can help you monitor your workouts and activities. Here's how to track your workouts and activities on your Apple Watch:

1. Open the Workout app on your Apple Watch Series 7.
2. Choose the type of workout you want to track, such as running, cycling, swimming, or strength training.
3. Set your goal for the workout, such as distance, time, or calorie burn.
4. Start your workout by tapping "Start."
5. During your workout, your Apple Watch will display real-time metrics, such as distance, pace, heart rate, and calorie burn.

6. When you're finished with your workout, swipe right and tap "End" to stop tracking.

In addition to tracking your workouts, your Apple Watch can also track your daily activities, such as steps taken, stairs climbed, and calories burned. Here's how to view your daily activity progress:

1. Open the Activity app on your Apple Watch Series 7.
2. Swipe left or right to view your progress towards your daily goals, such as standing, exercise, and move goals.
3. Tap on each ring to see more detailed information about your progress, such as the number of calories burned or the number of hours you've stood.

By tracking your workouts and activities on your Apple Watch Series 7, you can monitor your progress, set new goals, and improve your overall fitness level.

Heart rate monitoring

The Apple Watch Series 7 has a built-in heart rate monitor that can help you track your heart rate during workouts and throughout the day. Here's how to use the heart rate monitor on your Apple Watch:

1. Open the Heart Rate app on your Apple Watch Series 7.

2. Place your index finger on the Digital Crown and hold it there for a few seconds.
3. Wait for the heart rate reading to appear on the screen.
4. To view your heart rate throughout the day, open the Heart Rate app and tap on "All Data."

In addition to manual heart rate readings, your Apple Watch can also automatically track your heart rate during workouts and throughout the day. Here's how to set up automatic heart rate tracking:

1. Open the Watch app on your iPhone.
2. Tap on "My Watch" and then "Privacy."
3. Enable "Heart Rate" and "Fitness Tracking" if they're not already enabled.
4. Open the Heart Rate app on your Apple Watch and tap on "Set Up Heart Rate."
5. Follow the on-screen instructions to complete the setup.

By monitoring your heart rate on your Apple Watch Series 7, you can track your fitness progress, identify potential health issues, and make adjustments to your workout routine as needed.

Fall detection

The Apple Watch Series 7 has a fall detection feature that can detect when you take a hard fall and automatically contact emergency services if you don't respond within a set amount of time. Here's how to enable fall detection on your Apple Watch:

1. Open the Watch app on your iPhone.
2. Tap on "My Watch" and then "Emergency SOS."
3. Enable "Fall Detection" if it's not already enabled.

Once fall detection is enabled, your Apple Watch will use its sensors to detect when you take a hard fall. If a fall is detected, your Apple Watch will vibrate and display an alert asking if you're okay. If you don't respond within a set amount of time, your Apple Watch will contact emergency services and share your location with them.

Here are some tips for using fall detection on your Apple Watch Series 7:

1. Make sure your Apple Watch is snug on your wrist to ensure accurate fall detection.
2. If you take a fall and can't respond to the alert on your Apple Watch, emergency services will be contacted automatically.
3. If you're testing fall detection, make sure to turn off the automatic emergency call feature before you take a fall.
4. If you don't want to use fall detection, you can turn it off in the Watch app on your iPhone.

By enabling fall detection on your Apple Watch Series 7, you can have peace of mind knowing that you'll be automatically connected with emergency services if you're unable to respond after taking a hard fall.

ECG app

The Apple Watch Series 7 has a built-in ECG (electrocardiogram) app that can help you monitor your heart health by measuring the electrical activity of your heart. Here's how to use the ECG app on your Apple Watch:

1. Make sure your Apple Watch is snug on your wrist and in contact with your skin.
2. Open the ECG app on your Apple Watch Series 7.

3. Place your finger on the Digital Crown and hold it there for about 30 seconds.
4. Wait for the ECG reading to appear on the screen.

The ECG app on your Apple Watch can help you detect signs of atrial fibrillation, a type of irregular heartbeat that can increase your risk of stroke and other heart-related problems. If the ECG app detects an irregular heartbeat, it will notify you and recommend that you contact your doctor.

Here are some tips for using the ECG app on your Apple Watch Series 7:

1. The ECG app is not intended for use by people under the age of 22.
2. The ECG app is not a substitute for professional medical advice and should not be used to diagnose or treat any medical condition.
3. If you have a history of heart problems or other medical conditions, talk to your doctor before using the ECG app.
4. Make sure to follow the on-screen instructions carefully when using the ECG app.
5. The ECG app requires watchOS 7 or later and is not available in all regions.

By using the ECG app on your Apple Watch Series 7, you can monitor your heart health and detect potential issues early, allowing you to take action to protect your health.

Communication and Productivity Features

Making and receiving calls and texts

The Apple Watch Series 7 makes it easy to stay connected with your friends and family by allowing you to make and receive calls and texts right from your wrist. Here's how to use these features on your Apple Watch:

Making Calls:

1. Press the Digital Crown to access the Home screen.
2. Tap on the Phone app.
3. Scroll through your contacts and select the person you want to call.
4. Tap on the phone icon to initiate the call.
5. Speak into the built-in microphone and listen through the speaker or connected Bluetooth headphones.

Receiving Calls:

1. When someone calls you, you'll feel a tap on your wrist and hear a ringing sound.
2. To answer the call, swipe the green answer icon on the screen.
3. Speak into the built-in microphone and listen through the speaker or connected Bluetooth headphones.

Sending Texts:

1. Press the Digital Crown to access the Home screen.

2. Tap on the Messages app.
3. Select the person you want to text.
4. Use the Scribble feature or dictate your message using Siri.
5. Tap send when you're finished.

Receiving Texts:

1. When you receive a text message, you'll feel a tap on your wrist and hear a notification sound.
2. To read the message, raise your wrist or tap the screen.
3. To respond, use the Scribble feature or dictate your message using Siri.

With the Apple Watch Series 7, you can easily make and receive calls and texts without having to pull out your iPhone. This feature is especially convenient when you're on the go or in situations where pulling out your phone might be awkward or inconvenient.

Siri

Siri is Apple's intelligent voice assistant that is built into the Apple Watch Series 7. You can use Siri to control your Apple Watch, ask questions, and get things done without having to use your hands. Here's how to use Siri on your Apple Watch:

1. To activate Siri, raise your wrist or press and hold the Digital Crown until you hear a beep.

2. Once activated, you can ask Siri to do things like set reminders, send messages, make phone calls, and more.
3. To ask Siri a question or give a command, simply speak clearly into the built-in microphone.
4. After you've given your command or asked your question, Siri will respond with an answer or action.

Here are some tips for using Siri on your Apple Watch Series 7:

1. You can also activate Siri by saying "Hey Siri" if you have enabled this feature in the Apple Watch settings.
2. If you're having trouble getting Siri to understand you, try speaking more slowly and clearly.
3. You can customize Siri's settings to make it work more efficiently for you. For example, you can choose which language Siri uses or enable Voice Feedback so that Siri responds to you audibly.
4. Siri can also control your smart home devices, such as your lights or thermostat, if they are compatible with HomeKit.
5. If Siri is unable to perform a task or answer a question, it may suggest that you try the same command on your iPhone.

By using Siri on your Apple Watch Series 7, you can get things done quickly and easily, without having to use your hands. Whether you need to make a phone call, set a reminder, or get directions, Siri is there to help you out.

Email and messaging

The Apple Watch Series 7 makes it easy to manage your emails and messages directly from your wrist. Here's how to use these features:

Email:

1. Press the Digital Crown to access the Home screen.
2. Tap on the Mail app.
3. Scroll through your inbox and select the email you want to read.
4. Use the Digital Crown or swipe up and down to scroll through the email.
5. If you want to respond, tap the Reply button and use the Scribble feature or dictate your response using Siri.

Messaging:

1. Press the Digital Crown to access the Home screen.
2. Tap on the Messages app.
3. Select the person you want to message.
4. Use the Scribble feature or dictate your message using Siri.
5. Tap send when you're finished.

With the Apple Watch Series 7, you can easily manage your emails and messages on the go without having to pull out your iPhone. This feature is especially useful when you're in situations where you can't access your phone or when you need to respond quickly to an urgent message.

Calendar and reminders

The Apple Watch Series 7 allows you to stay organized with your calendar and reminders directly from your wrist. Here's how to use these features:

Calendar:

- Press the Digital Crown to access the Home screen.
- Tap on the Calendar app.
- Scroll through your calendar to view upcoming events.
- Tap on an event to view more details or to set a reminder for it.
- If you want to add a new event, tap the "+" icon and use the Scribble feature or dictate the details using Siri.

Reminders:

1. Press the Digital Crown to access the Home screen.
2. Tap on the Reminders app.
3. Scroll through your list of reminders.
4. Tap on a reminder to mark it as complete or to edit its details.
5. If you want to add a new reminder, tap the "+" icon and use the Scribble feature or dictate the details using Siri.

With the Apple Watch Series 7, you can easily stay on top of your schedule and tasks without having to constantly check your phone. This feature is especially useful when you're in meetings or on the go, and you need to quickly add or view your calendar events and reminders.

Apple Watch Apps

Overview of built-in apps

The Apple Watch Series 7 comes with a variety of built-in apps that make it easy to stay connected, organized, and healthy. Here's an overview of some of the most useful built-in apps:

- **Activity:** This app tracks your daily movement, exercise, and standing time, and helps you set and achieve fitness goals.
- **Workouts:** This app allows you to select and track a variety of workouts, including running, cycling, swimming, and more.
- **Messages:** This app lets you view and respond to text messages and iMessages directly from your wrist.
- **Phone:** This app allows you to make and receive phone calls directly from your watch, without having to use your iPhone.
- **Mail:** This app allows you to view and respond to emails directly from your wrist.
- **Maps:** This app provides turn-by-turn directions and real-time traffic updates, making it easy to navigate your way around town.
- **Siri:** This app allows you to use voice commands to perform a variety of tasks, such as sending a message, setting a reminder, or playing music.

- **Calendar:** This app allows you to view and manage your calendar events directly from your watch.
- **Reminders:** This app allows you to create and manage reminders directly from your wrist.
- **Stopwatch:** This app allows you to time events and activities.
- **Timer:** This app allows you to set a countdown timer for various tasks.
- **Alarms:** This app allows you to set alarms for various tasks and events.
- **Photos:** This app allows you to view and scroll through your photo library on your wrist.
- **Weather:** This app provides real-time weather updates and forecasts for your current location and other saved locations.
- **Calculator:** This app allows you to perform basic calculations directly from your watch.

These built-in apps are designed to provide convenience and functionality for your daily life, and you can customize them to suit your specific needs and preferences.

Downloading and installing third-party apps

In addition to the built-in apps, the Apple Watch Series 7 allows you to download and install third-party apps from the App Store. Here's how to download and install third-party apps on your Apple Watch:

1. Open the App Store app on your Apple Watch.
2. Browse or search for the app you want to download.
3. Once you've found the app, tap on it to view its details.
4. Tap the "Get" button to download the app. If the app is not free, you may need to authenticate the purchase with your Apple ID password or using Touch ID or Face ID.
5. Wait for the app to download and install on your watch. This process may take a few minutes, depending on the size of the app and your internet connection.
6. Once the app is installed, it should appear on your watch's Home screen.

To customize and manage your third-party apps, you can use the Watch app on your iPhone. Here's how:

1. Open the Watch app on your iPhone.
2. Tap on the "My Watch" tab at the bottom of the screen.
3. Scroll down to the "Installed on Apple Watch" section.
4. Tap on the app you want to customize or manage.
5. From here, you can enable or disable features such as notifications, complication placement, and Siri commands.
6. You can also rearrange the order of your apps on the Home screen by pressing and holding on an app icon until it jiggles, then dragging it to a new location.

Note that not all third-party apps may be optimized for the Apple Watch, and some may not work as well as others. Be sure to read reviews and check for compatibility before downloading any third-party apps.

Managing apps

Managing apps on your Apple Watch Series 7 is easy and can be done directly from your watch or your paired iPhone. Here are some ways you can manage your apps:

1. Rearranging apps on your watch face: Press and hold the app icon until it jiggles, then drag it to a new location on the watch face.
2. Removing apps from your watch: Press and hold the app icon until it jiggles, then tap the "x" button on the app icon and confirm that you want to delete the app.
3. Managing app notifications: Open the Watch app on your iPhone and tap the "Notifications" section. From here, you can customize the notifications for each app installed on your watch.
4. Adjusting app settings: Open the Watch app on your iPhone and tap on the "My Watch" tab. Scroll down to the "Installed on Apple Watch" section, tap on the app you want to customize, and adjust the settings as desired.
5. Updating apps: To update apps on your Apple Watch, open the App Store app on your watch and tap on the

"Updates" tab. If there are any available updates, tap "Update All" or update each app individually.

6. Offloading apps: If you want to free up space on your watch, you can offload apps. This will remove the app from your watch but keep its data saved on your iPhone. To offload an app, open the Watch app on your iPhone and tap on the app you want to offload. Toggle on the "Offload App" option.

With these simple steps, you can easily manage and customize the apps on your Apple Watch Series 7 to suit your preferences and needs.

Apple Pay

Setting up Apple Pay on the watch

Setting up Apple Pay on your Apple Watch Series 7 is a convenient way to make purchases without having to take out your wallet or phone. Here's how to set up and use Apple Pay on your watch:

1. Open the Watch app on your iPhone.
2. Tap on the "My Watch" tab at the bottom of the screen.
3. Scroll down and tap on "Wallet & Apple Pay."
4. Tap on "Add Card" and follow the on-screen instructions to add your debit or credit card to your watch.
5. If your card is already in your iPhone's Wallet, you can choose to add it automatically by tapping on "Add Next Card" and selecting your card.

6. Once your card is added to your watch, you can use it to make payments at any merchant that accepts Apple Pay.

To use Apple Pay on your Apple Watch:

1. Double-press the side button on your watch to bring up the Wallet app.
2. Swipe left or right to select the card you want to use for the purchase.
3. Hold your watch near the contactless payment terminal.
4. Wait for the "Done" and checkmark confirmation to appear on your watch screen.

Note that you will need to authenticate your payment with either your passcode or Touch ID/Face ID, depending on your watch settings. You can also set a default card for use with Apple Pay in the Watch app on your iPhone, and you can manage and remove cards from your watch in the "Wallet & Apple Pay" section of the Watch app.

Making payments

Making payments with your Apple Watch Series 7 is simple and convenient. With Apple Pay set up on your watch, you can make purchases without having to take out your wallet or phone. Here's how to make payments with your watch:

1. Double-press the side button on your watch to bring up the Wallet app.
2. Swipe left or right to select the card you want to use for the purchase.
3. Hold your watch near the contactless payment terminal.
4. Wait for the "Done" and checkmark confirmation to appear on your watch screen.

If your purchase requires a signature, you may be prompted to sign on the payment terminal screen. Some merchants may also require you to enter a PIN or provide a signature on the screen of your watch.

Note that you will need to authenticate your payment with either your passcode or Touch ID/Face ID, depending on your watch settings. You can also set a default card for use with Apple Pay in the Watch app on your iPhone, and you can manage and remove cards from your watch in the "Wallet & Apple Pay" section of the Watch app.

Keep in mind that not all merchants may accept Apple Pay, so it's always a good idea to have a backup payment method on hand, such as a physical credit or debit card.

Troubleshooting

Common issues and solutions

Here are some common issues you may encounter while using your Apple Watch Series 7, along with their solutions:

1. The watch won't turn on or respond.
   - Solution: If your watch is unresponsive, try restarting it by holding down the side button until the Apple logo appears. If this doesn't work, try force restarting the watch by holding down both the side button and the Digital Crown for about 10 seconds. If the problem persists, try resetting the watch to its factory settings.
2. The watch is not syncing with your iPhone.
   - Solution: Make sure that your watch and iPhone are within range of each other and that they are both connected to Wi-Fi or cellular data. Also, check that your watch and iPhone are running the latest software updates. If the problem persists, try unpairing and re-pairing your watch with your iPhone.
3. The battery is draining quickly.
   - Solution: Make sure that your watch is not running unnecessary apps in the background, and disable features like Always-On Display, Raise to Wake, and Noise Monitoring if you don't need them. You

can also adjust the brightness and haptic settings to conserve battery life. If the problem persists, try restarting your watch and iPhone, and make sure that your watch is not overheating.

4. The watch is not tracking your workouts accurately.
   - Solution: Make sure that your watch is properly secured on your wrist and that the sensors are in contact with your skin. Also, make sure that you have selected the correct workout type and that your watch is calibrated for your stride length and other measurements. If the problem persists, try resetting your watch's calibration data and recalibrating it.

5. The watch is not connecting to Wi-Fi or cellular data.
   - Solution: Make sure that your watch is within range of a Wi-Fi network or cellular signal, and that you have set up Wi-Fi or cellular data on your watch. Also, make sure that your watch and iPhone are both running the latest software updates. If the problem persists, try resetting your watch's network settings or contacting your carrier for assistance.

If you are still experiencing issues with your Apple Watch Series 7, you can contact Apple Support for further assistance.

Resetting the watch

If you're experiencing persistent issues with your Apple Watch Series 7, you may need to reset it to its factory settings. Here's how to do it:

1. On your watch, go to Settings > General > Reset.
2. Choose "Erase All Content and Settings" and enter your passcode if prompted.
3. Wait for the process to complete. This may take several minutes.

Note that resetting your watch will erase all of your data and settings, so be sure to back up your watch before resetting it if possible. You can do this by unpairing your watch from your iPhone, which will create a backup of your watch's data on your iPhone. To do this, go to the Watch app on your iPhone, tap on your watch, and choose "Unpair Apple Watch". You can then set up your watch as a new device or restore it from the backup you just created.

After resetting your watch, you'll need to set it up again and pair it with your iPhone. You can do this by opening the Watch app on your iPhone and following the on-screen prompts.

Conclusion

Summary of key features and benefits of the Apple Watch Series 7

Here's a summary of the key features and benefits of the Apple Watch Series 7:

1. Larger and brighter always-on Retina display.
2. Faster charging time and longer battery life.
3. Enhanced durability with a crack-resistant front crystal and IP6X certification.
4. New watch faces and customizations, including new watch bands and colors.
5. Advanced health monitoring features, such as ECG and blood oxygen tracking.
6. Wide range of fitness tracking features, including tracking for over 50 workout types.
7. Built-in cellular and Wi-Fi connectivity for phone calls, texts, and internet access.
8. Integration with Apple Pay for easy mobile payments.
9. Advanced Siri voice assistant functionality.
10. Compatibility with a wide range of third-party apps.

Overall, the Apple Watch Series 7 offers a range of advanced features and improvements over previous models, making it a versatile and convenient tool for health, fitness, communication, and more.

Final tips and recommendations

Here are some final tips and recommendations for using your Apple Watch Series 7:

1. Take advantage of the advanced health and fitness tracking features to monitor your overall wellbeing.
2. Customize your watch face and complications to fit your needs and preferences.
3. Experiment with different watch bands to find the most comfortable and functional fit.
4. Keep your watch up to date with the latest software updates to ensure optimal performance and security.
5. Use Siri and voice commands to simplify tasks and access information hands-free.
6. Protect your watch from damage by avoiding extreme temperatures, impacts, and exposure to water.
7. Explore the wide range of available apps and third-party integrations to find new ways to use your watch.

Overall, the Apple Watch Series 7 is a powerful and versatile tool that can help you stay connected, stay healthy, and simplify your daily routine. By taking advantage of its many features and customizations, you can make the most of your watch and enjoy all the benefits it has to offer.